INTERMEDIATE LOAN

THIS ITEM MAY BE BORROWED FOR

ONE WEEK ONLY

INTERMEDIATE LOANS ARE IN HEAVY DEMAND,
PLEASE RETURN OR RENEW

To renew, telephone:
01243 816089 (Bishop Otter)
01243 812099 (Bognor Regis)

Published in 2002

© Hannah Mortimer

ISBN 1 898873 25 9

British Library Cataloguing
A catalogue record for this book is available from the British Library.

Q/
Ed

Published by QEd, The ROM Building, Eastern Avenue,
Lichfield, Staffs. WS13 6RN
Web site: www.qed.uk.com
Email: orders@qed.uk.com

Acknowledgement to Howard Church.

Printed in the United Kingdom by Stowes (Stoke-on-Trent).

Contents

Introduction

Who this book is for

This book will be useful for early years educators working in a variety of early years settings: pre-schools, private nurseries, day nurseries and schools. It will also be helpful for individuals training on NVQ or pre-school diploma courses and of interest to childminders, parents and carers of children who have attention difficulties in their early years.

The *SEN Code of Practice*

In early 2002, early years settings were given the guidance of a revised *Special Educational Needs Code of Practice* issued by the DfES. This code gives guidance about how you can assess, plan and monitor any special educational needs in your settings. You are asked to make a graded response to SEN, planning approaches within your setting where appropriate, and seeking outside help if this becomes necessary. When you are working to meet children's needs within your setting, this is known as providing 'Early Years Action' (see Chapter Two). If you reach the point where outside professional support is needed to help you plan for and support the child, then this is known as 'Early Years Action Plus' (Chapter Three). In this book, you will read about how you can identify, plan for, support and monitor the needs of children who have significant difficulties in attending and concentrating. Some of these children may have been diagnosed as having 'Attention Deficit Hyperactivity Disorder' (ADHD) or 'Attention Deficit Disorder' (without hyperactivity, ADD). Having regard to the *SEN Code of Practice* is a requirement for settings registered with the Early Years Development and Childcare Partnerships to receive funding.

Although reference is made to the *SEN Code of Practice* for England, the approaches in this book will be equally applicable in other countries.

The Early Learning Goals

Early years settings are also required to deliver a broad and balanced early years curriculum to all children. The QCA *Curriculum Guidance for the*

5

Foundation Stage specifies early learning goals across six areas of learning: personal, social and emotional development; language and literacy; mathematical development; knowledge and understanding of the world; physical development; and creative development. These are goals that most children will be expected to have reached by the end of the foundation stage (from age three to the end of reception class, age five). There are also suggested 'stepping stones' to help settings plan the developmental route towards these goals. In this book, you will find ideas for achieving small stepping stones of learning for the child who has great difficulties in concentrating and paying attention.

Defining ADHD and ADD

ADHD and ADD are medical terms and psychiatrists have clear guidelines for diagnosing them. Although all young children usually have short attention spans and are often very active, there are some children who have significant difficulties when compared with their peers which affect:

- sustaining their attentions;
- controlling impulsive behaviour; and
- controlling their motor activity.

These difficulties can affect their learning, their behaviour and their developmental progress. Some children are inattentive but not hyperactive (ADD), some are extremely active (ADHD) and others still are both (AD/HD). We will use the general term AD/HD when talking about children with these diagnoses.

How to use this book

This book has been kept short and readable so that you can read the whole of it and obtain an overall view of the issues and approaches for children with attention difficulties. The author refers to 'children with attention difficulties' rather than to 'children with AD/HD' because, in practice, children are often still being assessed and diagnosed during the early years. It makes more practical sense to look at their *needs* (to build up attention and concentration and to improve looking, listening and behaviour) rather than to wait upon a *diagnosis*. In this way, early years practitioners can start upon the important role of supporting these children without the feeling that outside expertise is needed first in order to provide a label. We discuss this further in Chapter One when we consider identification, diagnosis and what you might observe in this group of children.

In Chapter Two, you will read about ways of offering practical support in early years settings: how you can collect information, develop and implement programmes and activities, write an individual education plan (IEP) and monitor the child's progress. Chapter Three describes the kinds of support that might be available from professionals outside of the setting and how you can work alongside them to help the child. Chapter Four deals with the delivery of the early years curriculum effectively with useful strategies for children with attention difficulties and answers questions about how to break tasks down, build up a child's concentration, stay positive and manage any challenging behaviour effectively.

Chapter Five deals with how your setting can work in partnership with parents. Living with a child who has difficulties in attending and concentrating can be a difficult time as there may well be problems with managing challenging or very impulsive behaviour. How can you offer support and ensure effective home-setting liaison? What home programmes might be helpful?

The book ends with a list of useful addresses and resources. There are support groups and organisations that can offer support to parents and also information to parents and professionals involved with children who have AD/HD. There are books that should be helpful for both professionals and parents. Finally, there are suggestions for books which children might enjoy sharing and which provide starting points for talking together about behaviour and feelings.

Chapter One

Children with attention difficulties

What you might observe

Children with AD/HD or attention difficulties may have some or many of these characteristics *to a much greater extent than other children of their age*. They:

- have attention difficulties that have persisted for more than six months in different situations;

- find it hard to listen to stories or to concentrate for more than a minute or so on any one play activity;

- find it hard to respond to spoken instructions, forgetting what you have said from one moment to the next;

- may behave impulsively, rushing into something without any thought of the consequences;

- might behave in an almost random manner until you step in to stop them, lacking any internal 'conscience' or control;

- might find it extremely difficult to sit still or to keep to their own spaces, especially when sitting on the floor or waiting in line;

- may seem almost 'driven' by high physical energy, always on the go, climbing, running, rushing, fiddling, touching, talking, shouting;

- may fail to build on their learning and play, continuing in a rather random and aimless manner;

- may have poor confidence and/or low self-esteem.

What the implications are for you

All this means that you are likely to find yourself very busy! You have perhaps found yourself reacting more and more frequently to calamities, spills, tumbles, clashes of will, and are now finding that you need to make active plans for 'getting one step ahead'. We will look at suggestions for doing this in the next chapter. You might also have found yourself working hard to extend the child's play so that you can move on from the 'butterfly' stage of flitting from one activity to the next. You might have been tempted to see the child as misbehaving, though, on reflection, have realised that the child really cannot help it. Either way, you will probably be feeling that it is time to apply some structured interventions.

Diagnosis and prevalence

In the past, the term 'hyperactivity' used to be applied to children who had severe problems in controlling their level of activity. There is still a medical label of 'hyperkinetic syndrome' as defined by the World Health Organisation. More recently, it became clear that there were some children for whom the core problem was their difficulty in sustaining their attentions. The broader concept of AD/HD was developed to describe children who have problems in impulsivity, poor concentration, and often poor self-esteem and confidence. Some professionals believe that as many as one in 20 children might be affected in some way. The conditions are recognised more widely in the USA. However, there is still controversy about using the label and around the whole issue of prescribing stimulant medication to children.

Diagnosis depends on a rigorous assessment in several situations. Children who have difficulties in attending, behaving or settling in just one situation (be it at home or in the more formal school/nursery setting) do not usually go on to receive this diagnosis. There will be many children who present in this way some of the time in some situations, and the approaches in this book will be relevant to them too. This leaves the way open for you to intervene on the basis of need rather than medical diagnosis. The emphasis of this book is on early years interventions, and you might wish to read further (see pages 39 and 40) if you wish to read more about the medical assessment and diagnosis of AD/HD.

Issues around medication

We still have much to research about AD/HD. At present, it is thought to be caused mainly by neurological dysfunction in which the brain is not exerting its usual controlling function. It seems that the neurotransmitters in the brain are less active than normal. This is why stimulant medication (such as Ritalin) is sometimes used in older children to treat the condition. Many NHS Trusts now have clearly defined protocols for diagnosing and treating AD/HD. The reason that medication is not generally available for younger children is that it has very different effects on different individuals. A child needs to have developed the introspection necessary for being able to report 'this is how it makes me feel'. Otherwise, we might fail to observe what can be quite unpleasant side effects for the child. Many doctors would not consider prescribing medication until the child is at least six.

Parents usually report that medication, when used regularly and at appropriate times of day, can make their children more able to concentrate, to learn and to settle. It does not provide a 'magic wand' for solving behaviour problems, but makes the child more able to respond to positive behaviour management. If a child is too young to receive medication, positive behaviour management approaches are still used to provide support to the child. For this reason they feature widely in this book. Readers might find the book *Developing Individual Behaviour Plans in Early Years* (Mortimer, 2000a) a helpful aid.

Dilemmas and challenges

There continues to be controversy about the diagnosis and treatment of AD/HD. Some of the dilemmas come from the fact that many of the characteristics of AD/HD also apply to children who have attachment difficulties or who have difficulties in behaving for whatever reason. When life with a young child is very challenging, it can be tempting and totally understandable to look for a label to describe the problem and to seek medicine to put it right. Unfortunately, we have no 'litmus test' as such to know definitely that our diagnosis is right, and we still depend on trying the medication and behaviour management approaches and seeing whether these work for child, parents and carers. It seems very clear that there is a population of children who have extreme and genuine difficulties in controlling their impulses, their attention and their level of activity. What we still need to perfect is our ability to spot and treat these children and to use the least intrusive treatment to ensure positive change.

Fortunately, we need not become preoccupied with these dilemmas in early years settings. The approach suggested here is that you identify needs and take steps to support the children and help them to progress along the lines of the *SEN Code of Practice*. This is why the rest of this book focuses on educational needs and approaches rather than medical diagnoses and prescriptions. In Chapter Three there is further information about how you can work alongside doctors and others to provide a multidisciplinary approach.

For this reason, we shall not talk about 'AD/HD children' so much as 'children with attention difficulties'. This allows you to focus on the behaviours presented as opposed to the medical label. This also allows you an early years 'way in' – and you are in familiar territory.

Chapter Two

Supporting children with attention difficulties: Early Years Action

Identification

We have already learned that children with AD/HD will not always be extremely active. This makes early identification rather more difficult than simply spotting an extremely active child who cannot settle. We also know that very young children are usually very active and have short attention spans, especially if they have not yet had the opportunities to develop play skills and concentration. So how can you identify the child who has difficulties that go above and beyond what is usual for their age?

In the early years, you may well live and work with children who go on to receive a diagnosis of AD/HD, but it is also likely that the diagnosis will not have been made just yet for all the reasons above. So the best approach will be a pragmatic one: if children need your extra planning and action to learn to concentrate and to settle when compared to their peers, then go ahead and plan. It is at the point where you begin to plan for all children on the basis of their *individual needs* (rather than on the basis of any medical label) that you are beginning to provide *inclusively*.

Young children with attention difficulties may find it harder than others to play for long on any one activity or plaything, *even when you have played alongside them and tried to extend their concentrations*. This happens *even when they are playing spontaneously* (in other words, it is not just a response to someone else's agenda). They may be extremely active, rushing around impulsively, never sitting still, jostling, touching and fiddling constantly *more than other children their age with their experiences*.

You may find it hard to engage them when you want to tell them something, and they appear 'selectively deaf' to your instructions. Perhaps your instructions do work but only for a second or two. They may 'flit' between activities far more than other children. They may be getting into trouble for physical rough-and-tumbling, for doing things impulsively, for not listening, or for not following the rules and routines of the setting. The difficulties you observe in the setting will be similar to those which parents tell you about at home. The child might be excessively dreamy and unaware of what is going on around them *yet can be engaged if you go up to them and break into the dreaminess.*

Collecting information

You will find the book *The Observation and Assessment of Children in the Early Years* (Mortimer, 2001a) helpful here. The two main starting points for your assessment will be to talk with parents and to observe the child in your setting.

Observations can take different forms. You might carry out a **fly on the wall observation**, observing a child over a period of time (say 30 minutes) and writing down what they are doing and how they are interacting in clear, unambiguous terms. Ask colleagues to handle the children in exactly the same way as they usually would and not to rely on you, the observer, to intervene. You might also use a **timed observation** by noting what a child is doing, say, every five minutes regardless of what is happening in the setting. Are they still playing appropriately? We might involve the child in an activity and make a **participant observation** of what the child does and how they interact and learn with us. **On the spot observations** involve the adult noting down significant events or achievements after they happen in a kind of running diary. If you are trying this, then make sure you record positive occasions when you all felt really pleased with the child's achievements as well as the difficult times. This provides you with far more information about what actually 'works' for the child. After all, remember that your assessment is done in order to lead to positive change for the child and not just to tell people how difficult things are.

When observing a child whom you feel has attention difficulties, it is useful to choose a second child of a similar age, stage and experience with whom to compare them. Is the child's behaviour really so different? Here is

13

an example of the sort of questions you should be asking and the observations you should be making.

Is Ruben's behaviour extremely active, impulsive or challenging both at home and in your setting? Once settled in, does he show only short-lived signs of responding to your group's routines and rules; is this similar at home? Does he seem to be very dreamy, quiet and withdrawn, even once he has had a chance to settle in with familiar adults and familiar children? What seems to help? Your observations should give you an idea of what led up to the child's particularly inattentive behaviour, what the child is actually doing that seems different from the other children, and what effect the interventions you were trying had on the child.

Talking with parents

Children who have significant difficulties in attending and concentrating also tend to show behaviour which is challenging both for parents and early years educators alike. It is all too easy for the first contacts between setting and home to provoke feelings of defensiveness and hostility ('Are they saying that my child has problems?' 'Do they feel that this is because I have been a bad parent?').

By the time you have decided that 'something must be done', staff and parents may already be feeling stressed that their usual approaches have not worked for the child in question and that this might reflect on their teaching or their parenting. So how can staff ensure that their communication with the parents of children with attention difficulties is positive, mutually useful and productive?

It is helpful to understand the cycle of defensiveness that parents and staff can get into. If you have formed some kind of positive relationship with parents based on a warm welcome to your setting, clear information about what you do and mutual respect for the roles each of you play *before* problems have to be talked about, this can be extremely helpful. Invest time before the child starts in visits and welcome sessions. Make it clear that parents are welcomed and an important part of what you do by using regular newsletters and opportunities for contact. Phrase your questions positively and make it clear that you both have an identical aim; to help their child feel settled and to benefit from the early learning opportunities you provide.

The questions 'What do you do when you really want him to concentrate at home?' or 'What helps her settle down at home?' both share the problem but also respect the parents for the advice they can give you. The statement 'We think your child has a problem' leads nowhere and can leave the listener feeling powerless, deskilled and demoralised. Start by emphasising the child's strengths ('He's really good at climbing and is beautifully co-ordinated ...'), lead into the weaknesses ('... but we must find ways of helping him to settle and concentrate when we are talking in a group ...') and finish with what you can both do about it ('... so we are going to start by helping him listen to stories with one adult and then help him cope in a larger group. Can you look through books together at home too?') These ideas will be further developed Chapter Five.

How to develop and implement programmes and activities

One of the characteristics of providing Early Years Action for any child with SEN in your setting is that you will produce an individual education plan which you will negotiate and share with parents and colleagues. This IEP is usually drawn up by the special educational needs co-ordinator (SENCO). The plan specifies what you feel the child's needs are, what you will do to help, how you will involve parents and how you will monitor the child's progress. You will find an example of an IEP on page 16 and ideas for strategies that are helpful for designing an individual programme of activities in Chapter Four.

Individual Education Plan

Name: Ruben   **Early Years Action**

Nature of Difficulty

Ruben is very active and finds it hard to sit still, to look, to listen and to concentrate. He enjoys physical play but this can quickly become over-enthusiastic and he can sometimes hurt others.

Action

1. Seeking further information   Who will do what?

Parents have asked for him to be referred to the Child and Family Service through their health visitor. They have given us permission to contact the child psychologist, Heather S.

Marie, SENCO

2. Seeking training or support

We will contact our Area SENCO for more information about helping children with attention difficulties and AD/HD. Are there any courses available?   Marie, SENCO

3. Observations and assessments

We will conduct 'fly on the wall' observations at different times of the session over the next month. We will observe him both in structured play-times and in free play. We will write a list of 'strengths' and 'weaknesses' which will help our planning.

Suli, play-leader

4. Managing the behaviour

What exactly is the inappropriate behaviour we wish to change?

Ruben flits from activity to activity. He quickly gets into play fights. He can kick and squeeze other children.

What behaviour do we wish to encourage instead?

We want Ruben to concentrate for longer and show less physical aggression.

What will we do in general to make appropriate behaviour more likely to occur?

Tom, keyworker, will play alongside Ruben and one other chosen child for five minutes each session to encourage the play.

Ruben will be watched closely and distracted as soon as he begins to become 'physical'.

We will show Ruben how to share toys, play appropriately with a partner and ask for things.

What will we do whenever the inappropriate behaviour happens?

We will engage his eye contact, say a clear 'no kicking', remove him from the situation, distract him with a new activity, support him and then praise him for playing appropriately.

What will we do whenever the appropriate behaviour happens instead?

We will use high levels of praise and encouragement.

Help from parents

Ruben's parents will engage his eye contact and use his name whenever they need to tell or ask him something.

Targets for this term

1. We want Ruben to play for up to five minutes on a favourite activity (e.g. the train) when an adult plays close by.

2. We want Ruben to stop kicking and squeezing other children.

3. We want Ruben to listen to, remember and carry out a simple one-act instruction (e.g. please do this ...).

How will we measure whether we have achieved these?

Regular observations each half-term.

Review meeting with parents

Within the first three weeks of next term.

Who else to invite

The health visitor. The child psychologist (if available).

Monitoring progress

Once you have agreed an IEP, choose activities that are going to help you achieve these targets and keep records so that you can see how effective you have been. In this way, you will have information to report back on at the next review. Review should be at least every term for early years children since their needs change so rapidly. You might choose to supplement your play activities with a behavioural programme for managing difficult behaviour and again you will find the books on pages 39 and 40 helpful. The idea is that your interventions should arise from your planning and be influenced by your monitoring so that you build up a smooth 'plan – intervene – monitor – review' cycle.

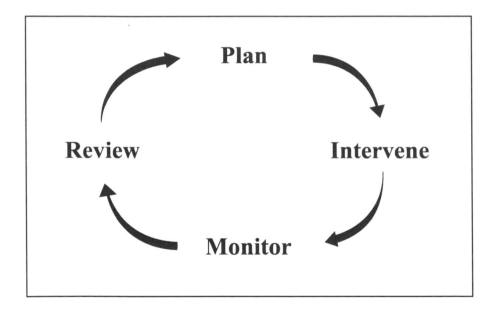

You will find some useful strategies to include in your interventions in Chapter Four. Sometimes, you will find yourselves needing more support and advice in order to meet a child's needs. This is where you might plan Early Years Action Plus which involves building in assessment and advice from other outside professionals. This is covered in the next chapter.

Chapter Three

Early Years Action Plus for children with attention difficulties

When to seek help

Sometimes there comes a time when all kinds of interventions have been carried out and monitored in the setting and you still feel that the child is not making significant progress or that their needs are not being met. This is the stage when you might request additional assessment and support from outside the setting. This is known as taking Early Years Action Plus. However, as far as the setting is concerned, this does not mean that you will not have been doing something to help already at the Early Years Action phase (see Chapters Two and Four).

Whether or not the child goes on to receive a diagnosis of AD/HD or continues to need support via an outside professional or even statement of SEN (see page 24), you will still have identified that the child needs help to build up their concentration and attention and have been working to do this. Hence the use of the terminology 'attention difficulties' in this book. It is quite often during this Early Years Action Plus phase that an outside professional might consider a diagnosis of AD/HD but, in one sense, this proceeds separately to all the good work you should already be doing in the setting. The arrival of the *diagnosis* does not change the child's *needs*.

Working with other professionals

What might happen in the Early Years Action Plus phase? There are two main scenarios. Perhaps parents or carers have been concerned about their child's behaviour for some time and already have sought help, probably through the NHS services. On the other hand, perhaps you are identifying a child's difficulties within the setting and you and parents together have decided that you need more support and advice through the setting's SEN support services.

In this first scenario, it is most likely that parents will have discussed their concerns with their GP or health visitor. Perhaps they have talked with other families, seen television programmes or read articles in magazines or in the press. Perhaps they are already feeling that the picture of AD/HD fits their child and their situation and they are seeking confirmation of this diagnosis. This can sometimes add complications to the process of diagnosis, since feelings and expectations might already be high. We have already talked about how children can show similar patterns of behaviour for different reasons.

The GP or health visitor is likely to seek more information and, depending on whether they feel that it would be helpful, might decide to refer the child to a child and family centre or to a consultant community or hospital paediatrician. They might then be assessed by a specialist doctor or clinical psychologist. Some children are also referred to dieticians for advice on managing their diet differently if this is felt to be affecting their behaviour and attention.

It is good practice for the professional to seek information about the child's behaviour in more than one situation and so this is the point where you might well be asked to send in information about the child's learning and behaviour in your setting. Quite often this is via a structured questionnaire. You will not necessarily be kept in touch with the assessment, since this is a medical and confidential process. However, parents could keep you informed if you have established a good working relationship with them. The Health Service also has a duty to inform the LEA if the child might have SEN. If you *can* liaise with the outside professional so as to build their recommendations and advice into the individual education plan for the child, then you are effectively working in the Early Years Action Plus phase.

If you yourselves are seeking help, then it will be from the support services which are available to your setting. Your SENCO should have already identified who these people are and what your normal route for contacting them is. Usually this involves some kind of referral form,

21

countersigned by parents to show that you have conferred together. It usually requires you sending in 'evidence' of what needs you have already identified in your Early Years Action, how you planned to meet these and how effective your approaches have been. This helps the outside professional decide on the priority of the referral and to have an idea of how special or severe the child's needs might be. It is also helpful to attach reports from all the review meetings you will have held with parents.

If an assessment is carried out by an outside support professional, it is most likely to be an early years support teacher, a behaviour support teacher or an educational psychologist. They should then produce advice for you to build into the child's individual education plan which you will review regularly with parents or carers. It is still your responsibility to meet the child's needs and to plan and monitor the approaches. The involvement of the outside professional does not mean that there is now 'someone else dealing with it'. However, it does mean that you should now have someone on hand to advise and support you in the help you are providing.

Gathering evidence

The outside professional who is providing the assessment might ask you for further information about the child's learning and behaviour in your setting. Sometimes this is so that the child's behaviour in the setting and at home can be compared. We have already seen that, if a diagnosis of AD/HD is to be made, the child needs to show long-term and significant difficulties in more than one situation. Some professionals like you to complete a standard checklist of information so that the answers can be compared with 'norms' for the child's age and stage, and that this can help with the diagnosis. This is because these checklists have been used on many children and the specialists can identify patterns of behaviour which seem to fit the cluster of children with AD/HD. One of these checklists widely used is the *Conners Teacher Rating Scale* (The Psychological Corporation).

What kind of questions might you be asked? You could use this framework for providing background information when you seek outside help.

- How does the child cope when you are all sitting quietly? Is the child more restless (always moving and fidgeting) than other children that age?

- How long does the child play on each activity? Is this affected by how interested they are in it? (Consider carrying out an observation, see page 13, noting the length of time on each play activity.) Do they flit quickly from one activity to another, even when you play alongside them to direct and encourage them?

- Do they find it hard to listen to short stories? Is this even when you are giving individual attention? Is it easier for the child when there is no background noise or when you have withdrawn to a quiet distraction-free space?

- Does the child find it hard to respond to spoken instructions, forgetting what you have said from one moment to the next? Is this even when you have used their name, established eye contact, emphasised a few simple keywords and asked them to repeat them?

- Does the child behave impulsively, rushing into something without any thought of the consequences? Is this even in very familiar situations in which you have gone over the rules and routines many times? Is it more so when the child is tired/excited/upset/in a new situation (i.e. look for the antecedents which lead up to the behaviour)?

- Does the child behave in an almost random manner until you intervene, lacking any internal 'conscience' or control? Does the child's behaviour improve when you use strong praise and behaviour management approaches (see page 28)?

- Does the child find it extremely difficult to sit still or to keep to their own space, especially when sitting on the floor or waiting in line? What have you already tried and how effective was this?

- Does the child daydream a lot? Can you attract their attention again if you really need to?

- Does the child seem almost 'driven' by high physical energy, always on the go, climbing, running, rushing, fiddling, touching, talking, shouting?

- Does the child fail to build on their learning and play, continuing in a rather random and aimless manner? What is your evidence for this?

If you are requesting outside help because a child's behaviour has become very difficult to manage, it is helpful to send in evidence of the behaviour management approaches you have already tried (see page 28). List the situations when the difficult behaviour is most likely to occur in the setting. It might be:

- while arriving at the setting;

- when separating from a parent or carer;

- during large/small group time;

- in highly structured/free play activities;

- when outside/inside;

- going to the toilet and washroom;

- in front of an 'audience'/when no-one is looking;

- during activities/in between activities;

- when doing table work/when playing physically;

- when listening/looking/moving.

A more formal assessment

Sometimes (and only for about 2% of all children in all educational settings), special educational needs are so great that the school or setting cannot meet them or ensure progress through Action Plus. For these children, there are local procedures which the SENCO should know about for asking the LEA to consider initiating a 'statutory assessment of SEN'. Again, you would be asked for all your evidence and parents and outside professionals would be consulted too. If the LEA decides that it has the evidence to proceed, then it will collect formal reports from those involved through a tightly defined legal procedure with tight timescales (six months overall). It might decide to draw up a 'statement of SEN' if the assessments warrant it, and the LEA then plays the roles of monitoring the needs and providing any additional resources necessary to meet the child's needs. In some cases this might involve extra support from a Personal Support Assistant (PSA) in the setting, though this is not always in the child's interests.

Chapter Four

Delivering the early years curriculum effectively

Useful strategies for children with attention difficulties

Children with short attention spans benefit from clear routines and structures so that they know what is going to happen and when. If attention is short, then these children sometimes find it helpful to 'sandwich' short periods of sustained concentration and effort with periods of time when they can be more active or have a free choice in their play. The best approach is therefore to start with very short periods of 'structured' activity, moving step by small step towards periods of longer concentration. Very strong encouragement and praise is needed to keep this fun, attention-getting and motivating for the child.

Try to avoid repetitive tasks which might become boring. Although it is helpful to have the general daily routine predictable and 'safe', look for new and interesting ways of playing and learning within that structure which are going to have an element of novelty and stimulation.

Breaking tasks down

Try to break tasks down into simpler steps so that the child with a short attention span can still play and learn from them. Keep your demands on the child short and simple to begin with; it might be a major step for the child to do *anything* that is not from their own agenda to begin with and this should be celebrated. Use your praise and your encouragement constantly to show the child that they are playing well.

Children with attention difficulties benefit greatly from the chance to talk with you ahead of any activity, to plan it together and then to review what they have done and how it worked afterwards. This use of 'plan – do – review' helps them to think about and engage with their learning which, in turn, helps the child to be less impulsive and more reflective.

Concentration is likely to be easiest for children with attention difficulties when playing in pairs rather than in a large group. In this way, they do not become over-stimulated and distracted. Often, their social skills are poor and there can be too many demands placed on them when having to cope in a large group.

Building up concentration

Children with attention difficulties may have a greater need than most children for distraction-free space to work in for activities that require sustained concentration, looking or listening. Try to have a quiet area which you can withdraw to with a small group of children and use this *before* difficulties with behaviour arise rather than as a reaction to them.

As highlighted earlier, these children are often very prone to distraction and you will find that they cope best if you plan carefully around reducing as many distractions as possible. Think of how you can provide quietness, but also areas without too many visual distractions, interesting views from windows, other classes at work etc. You will not wish the child to be isolated from distraction for all of the time, but this will allow you to choose the best work and play area for each activity you are planning.

They may also be very distracted by their own thoughts. Daydreaming can become a problem when it gets in the way of looking, listening and concentrating. Therefore, the activity that you are encouraging the child to do must be especially motivating and your constant encouragement might be needed to help the child stay 'on task' and to enjoy what they are doing.

Look at how long the child can concentrate at present and aim to build this up, step by small step, until the child can concentrate independently for a short period on something of their choosing. Later, you can extend this to short tasks of your choosing. Make sure you have eye contact before you speak to the child and use their name to get attention. Give very clear, short and concrete directions, showing the child what to do as well as telling. Ask them to repeat back what you have said and praise them for remembering.

Sometimes, children with attention difficulties have great difficulties in understanding time sequences and also sequencing information. Talk about the time of day and introduce familiar times on the clock ('At 10 o'clock we have drinks ... at 12 o'clock we go home', etc). Talk about what happened yesterday, today, and what will happen tomorrow. Cut up picture stories and play at arranging these in sequence. Use a picture board to put up simple pictures representing what will happen during the session.

Staying positive

Do not be surprised if you have to give reminders constantly since the child might forget your instructions readily. Try not to lose patience with the child; you might feel exasperated that you have to do so, but then you have already recognised that the child does have a genuine difficulty in attending so this should not be a surprise to you. Small and immediate rewards and praise are much more effective than larger rewards given at the end of a session. You can use favourite activities as effective rewards: 'When you have finished your puzzle, you can go on the computer ...'

Always stay calm when you address any difficult behaviours, keeping your language simple and clear. If you become cross or upset, it will only stir the child up further and make it more difficult for them to think logically and rationally about controlling their behaviour. If the child needs time to 'cool off', find somewhere quiet to withdraw to and give minimal attention until the child is calm again and ready for you to talk together about what happened.

Use your own running commentary as the child plays to hold their attention on what they are doing and to show that you value and are interested in their actions. This is far more effective than constant questioning.

Managing challenging behaviour

'Behaviour Management' is a useful tool when planning changes in difficult behaviours. Because children with attention difficulties find it hard to concentrate and attend, they often behave very impulsively and lack the social skills needed for social play and two-way 'give and take'. 'Behavioural' approaches are based on the use of rewards and punishments (or 'sanctions'). It is important for us to be clear in our definition of these before we start. You will find more information in *Developing Individual Behaviour Plans in Early Years Settings* (Mortimer, 2000a) and *Personal, Social and Emotional Development of Children in the Early Years* (Mortimer, 2001b).

In essence, a behavioural theory states that:

- If we do something, and something *pleasant* happens to us, we are more likely to do that thing again.

- If we do something, and something *unpleasant* happens to us, we are less likely to do that thing again.

- The *pleasant* event is called a *'reward'*, simply because it makes the behaviour *increase*.

- The *unpleasant* event is called a *'punishment'*, simply because it makes the behaviour *decrease*.

- A punishment need not be something that is 'given'. It could be that the child, expecting a certain reward, no longer gets it (e.g. the lashing out did not bring the expected tractor ride, or the tantrum did not lead to being able to play on the slide).

Gather information

Your next task is to gather more information about the difficult behaviour itself. Use one of the observation methods on page 13 to collect information about the difficult behaviours of the child. You might end up with several behaviours which you feel you ought to try to change. Select just one behaviour to work on first, one that is easy to change or one that is causing most disruption.

Now that you have information on the antecedents (what led up to that behaviour) and on the consequences (what happened to the child as a

29

result), you will be in a position to look for patterns in the child's behaviour and to decide on a hypothesis (what do you think is keeping that behaviour going?). You might be right, or you might be wrong, but it will give you the opportunity to devise a plan for intervention which you can then evaluate and redesign if you seem to be on the wrong track. With children who have attention difficulties, you may be feeling that many of the difficulties are caused by the child having a very short attention span, not looking or listening, or behaving impulsively rather than thinking about what they are doing.

Draw up a plan

You can now draw up a plan to change the *antecedents, behaviours* or *consequences.*

Changing the antecedents

This simply means that you try to avoid situations where the 'problem' behaviour is likely to occur. If a child cannot sit still during a group discussion, you might decide it is best to avoid that situation for the time being while you concentrate on teaching them to talk with one adult in the quiet corner. You can also try distracting the child rather than confronting them all the time. Make sure the activity and what you are asking the child to do suits the child's level. Young children with short attentions find it hard to realise that instructions given to a whole group also mean them, so cue individual children in first to what you are about to say.

Give a warning of changes of activity such as: 'In five minutes it will be time to go outside.' Try to anticipate problem times and be a step ahead. Keep a 'flow' between activities so that children are not waiting around. Children with difficulties in attention will find sitting still for long periods challenging, and find it easiest if they can sandwich 'doing' and 'letting off steam'.

Anticipate 'dangerous' impulsive behaviours by fixing safety locks on a yard gate or a 'stable gate' on a kitchen door. Providing a keyworker to monitor the child carefully and intervene at the right moment might prevent escalation of aggressive behaviour.

Changing the behaviours

Give clear directions. We know that children need full reasons and explanations if they are to learn about their worlds, yet there may be times when that is not appropriate. Choose what you want to say: 'No biting' and repeat that over, making your rule simple and clear. Sometimes, when an instruction does not work, we tend to say it in a different way or elaborate it with more detailed explanations. The more you elaborate, the more attention you are giving the child for behaving inappropriately and the less the child with short attention will hear.

Choose a few simple rules and stick to them. These are especially useful when your children have contributed to them too, perhaps as a 'circle time' activity (see books on pages 39 and 40). Try to stick to three to four rules at the most, perhaps relating to not hurting others, to being 'kind' and to listening. Take time to talk together about what it means to be 'kind' and to 'help'.

Changing the consequences

Try to make sure that you are all being absolutely consistent in how you manage the behaviour. You can also make sure that you reward when the child is not doing the inappropriate behaviour. Watch out for examples of appropriate behaviour to praise and encourage regularly. Try to make it *fun* to behave appropriately. Behaving in a certain way might have become quite a *habit* for that child and you will need to make your rewards and praise particularly *strong* to break the pattern. Make sure that your praise is attention-getting, strong for that child, immediate and easy to use (a trip with Mum or Dad much later on is not).

Star charts and stickers can sometimes work well. You will find some useful resources on page 40. Do not overuse these. Make sure the child knows exactly why they have earned a sticker (not just because they were 'good' or 'not naughty'). Never remove it once given, whatever the child does next. Stickers are a concrete sign that the child behaved in an appropriate way at that particular moment, and help them to learn that you have praised them because *they did something*, not because *you* decided to be pleased with them.

Summary of approaches

- Have a familiar routine and structure for the session, perhaps using a series of pictures or symbols to help the child predict what happens next.

- Break new activities down into smaller steps so that the child can concentrate and complete each thing successfully. Do one thing at a time.

- Have a small distraction-free area where you can go together to look through picture books or play quietly.

- 'Sandwich' short structured activities with periods of free play and more energy. Gradually build up the child's concentration, step by small step.

- Keep what you are saying to the child simple and brief. Before you speak, use their name and a light shoulder touch.

- If you are about to speak to the whole group, warn the child first and check afterwards that they have heard.

- Use frequent rewards and praise to reassure the child. Make sure their self-esteem remains positive.

- Work in small groups or with just one other child, supporting and praising the child's attempts at interaction, sharing and turn-taking.

- Patiently repeat any instructions that the child has forgotten.

- Word your comments carefully. Avoid words like 'good' and 'naughty', but use words that describe what you would like the child to do: 'Thank you for passing that to Lee'; 'Please climb down.'

- Try to form a positive and supportive relationship with the family; they are likely to be finding life difficult at home too. You will find more ideas for doing this in the next chapter.

Chapter Five

Working in partnership with parents

A difficult time

In his book *Attention Deficit Hyperactivity Disorder: Recognition, Reality and Resolution*, Dr Kewley (2001) describes AD/HD as a 'hidden handicap' since it is so often seen as a wilful problem of self-control rather than as a disability. Parents who suspect difficulties are often told to 'wait and see', though without support the child's difficulties can become worse. He suggests certain analogies for explaining the effects of AD/HD to parents; it can be like a car battery running flat so that the electrical signals do not get through smoothly; a radio tuned just off the correct channel so that messages do not get through clearly; or a car whose brakes do not work effectively making it difficult to stop.

The likelihood is that, if you are seeing that the child has considerable difficulties in attending and focusing in the setting, there are probably similar difficulties at home as well if the child has attention difficulties. Remind parents that they are not on their own. Simply showing the parents or carers that you 'understand' that the child has genuine difficulties and that you do not see the child as being wilfully 'naughty' can be a great support to them.

Gathering information

It is helpful to have a list of questions to ask parents or carers. This will help you decide whether the child's difficulties are evident both at home as well as in the setting. It will also assist in sharing together a picture of the child's strengths and weaknesses and planning together ways of supporting the child's early learning and behaviour. Here is a list of suggested questions:

- Is your child 'always on the go?' Have you linked this to anything (for example, to when the child has eaten certain things, when they have been kept indoors for a while, when they play 'rough and tumble' and then become overexcited)? What has helped at home?

- Does your child make friends easily? Can the child be friendly towards other children? Are you worried the child might be being teased? At home, can the child understand when he/she has to share or take turns?

- Is your child very restless? When he/she watches TV, can he/she sit still or is he/she always fidgeting? Does he/she settle at night-time?

- Is your child confident? Does your child worry about things that are going to happen, or does he/she tend to rush into things without thinking?

- Would you say your child got into more trouble than other children that age? If so, why do you think that is?

- Do you think your child is 'naughty', or are there real difficulties in knowing how to behave? What has helped at home?

- If you really needed your child to attend and listen to you, what would you do?

- Can your child follow simple instructions (such as 'go to your bedroom and fetch your slippers')? Can you think of a time when your child really surprised you by listening and remembering something quite complicated?

- Does your child become frustrated very easily? What does this make them do?

Having this kind of open-ended framework makes it much easier to lead into any talk about 'behaviour problems'. Ask the questions in a way that leaves it open for parents to reply in either direction (asking 'Is she toilet trained yet?' implies that she ought to be by now). Always listen and respect the answers you are given, and convey that you are genuinely interested in the information you are asking for. In other words, try not to seem judgemental; listen and receive.

Offering support

These general support strategies should be helpful at home as well as in the setting.

- Parents should praise the child frequently and straight away if they are behaving appropriately.

- It is best if you do not spend time cross-examining the child as to why they did something; the child might not always know and it can hurt sensitive feelings.

- Stick to routines. This provides predictability for the child and means that there is less for them to remember.

- Keep instructions clear and offer one at a time.

- Stay as calm as possible when dealing with difficult behaviour.

- Do not spend time reasoning or negotiating: be calm, clear, firm and predictable.

- Avoid difficult times and plan around them (such as not taking the child to a crowded supermarket unless it cannot be avoided).

- Do not use physical punishment. It does not work effectively and can actually become a challenge to the child.

Home-setting liaison

If you are going to have effective and productive liaison between home and setting, then you need to look at proactive ways of making this happen. First, you need to build up a basic respect for each other. You hope that parents and carers will acknowledge that you have something positive to offer their children. You in turn need to acknowledge the fundamental role that parents or carers have already played in their child's education. Look for ways of sharing the learning between home and setting by providing regular information, ideas sheets and newsletters.

Make sure that parents and carers feel welcome in your setting and that there are opportunities for working together. Make your admission procedures flexible to allow time for discussion with parents and carers and for children to feel secure in a new setting. If you already have an ongoing relationship with parents, then it makes it so much easier to talk about problems as they arise.

Home programmes

One useful way of supporting parents or carers of a child with attention difficulties is to negotiate a 'play plan' to share with them. This contains ideas for supporting their child's learning and behaviour at home and it can link in with the child's individual education plan (see page 16). Be sensitive to the way in which parents usually communicate, and use an interpreter if you need to, or even consider a project for linking parents and carers together for support.

This example is a play plan for Ruben, the little boy whom we have already met on page 14. The first sheet is shared with parents or carers who take it home and try out the ideas. The second sheet has their comments on how well Ruben managed the tasks, which they bring back to share with the setting.

Play Plan for Ruben

Play helps Ruben to look, listen and concentrate.

Getting started

Help Ruben to play for longer with you. Let him choose what he wants to play with and you play with him too for at least ten minutes each in the early evening. Play somewhere where it is quiet and there are not too many distractions. Do it when his little sister is in bed. Give lots of praise and show him how pleased you are.

When you need to speak to him, say his name and go up to him. Ask him to look at you. Say it very simply (two or three words at the most). If he still does not listen, go with him and help him do what you have asked. Again, praise him warmly.

Games to play

1. Construction and car games: using bricks and fitting pieces which Ruben can easily manage.
2. Give Ruben a chart to show how many times he listened to what you said. Add a sticker to it for each success.
3. Point out interesting things to see on bus journeys and walks.
4. Share picture books together – we will lend you some.

How to help

As Ruben becomes more able to concentrate, reduce the amount of help you give until he is managing to play a little bit all by himself, so long as you are nearby.

Parents and carers might also find it helpful to talk with their health visitor about diet or contact a support group for more help or general information. There are some addresses in the next section and also a list of information books, many of which are helpful for parents or carers as well as for early years educators. Think of books that you can share with the children too; these can provide starting points for talking about the child's own views, feelings and wishes.

References

DfES (2001) *Special Educational Needs Code of Practice*. London: HMSO.

Kewley, G.D. (2001) *Attention Deficit Hyperactivity Disorder: Recognition, Reality and Resolution*. London: David Fulton Publishers

Mortimer, H. (2000a) *Developing Individual Behaviour Plans in Early Years*. Tamworth: NASEN.

Mortimer, H. (2000b) *The Music Makers Approach: Inclusive Activities for Young Children with Special Educational Needs*. Tamworth: NASEN.

Mortimer, H. (2001a) *The Observation and Assessment of Children in the Early Years*. Lichfield: QEd Publications.

Mortimer, H. (2001b) *Personal, Social and Emotional Development of Children in the Early Years*. Lichfield: QEd Publications.

Qualifications and Curriculum Authority (QCA) (2000) *Curriculum Guidance for the Foundation Stage*. Hayes: QCA Publications.

Useful resources

Brainwaves (reward sticker albums, etc.), Trewithan Parc, Lostwithiel, Cornwall PL22 0BD.

Cooper, P. and Ideus, K. (1996) *Attention Deficit/Hyperactivity Disorder: a practical guide for teachers*. London: David Fulton Publishers.

The Magination Press specialises in books that help young children deal with personal or psychological concerns. Send for a catalogue from The Eurospan Group, 3 Henrietta Street, Covent Garden, London WC2E 8LU.

Mental Health Foundation (2000) *All About ADHD*. London: Mental Health Foundation.

Merrett, F. (1997) *Positive Parenting*. Lichfield: QEd Publications.

Mortimer, H. (2000) *The Music Makers Approach: Inclusive Activities for Young Children with Special Educational Needs*. Tamworth: NASEN.

Mosley, J. (1998) *More Quality Circle Time*. Cambridge: LDA.

Mosley, J. (1999) *Circle Time Kit* (puppets, rainstick, magician's cloak and many props for making circle time motivating). Cambridge: LDA.

Stenhouse, G. (1994) *Confident Children: Developing your Child's Self-esteem*. Oxford: Oxford University Press.

Super Stickers (for reward and motivation) from P.O. Box 55, 4 Balloon Avenue, Bangor, Co. Down, BT19 7PJ.

Books for children

Fraser's Grump by Sue Heap (published by Julia MacRae): a little boy goes into a 'grump' but comes out of it in time for tea.

The Second Princess by Hiawyn Oram and Tony Ross (Anderson Press): sibling rivalry and sharing.

Where the Wild Things Are by Maurice Sendak (Bodley Head): a classic story on the theme of mischief.

There's a dragon at my school by Jenny Tyler and Philip Hawthorn (Usborne Books): a helpful story for talking about rules.

The Writers' Press, USA, publishes a number of books for young children about a range of special educational needs (www.writerspress.com).

Organisations and support groups

ADHD Family Support Group, 1A High Street, Dilton Marsh, Westbury, Wiltshire BA14 4DL.

The ADHD National Alliance, 209–211 City Road, London EC1V 1JN (a support group started by **Contact a Family** in response to the large demand for information).

The Association of Workers for Children with Emotional and Behavioural Difficulties (AWCEBD), Charlton Court, East Sutton, Nr. Maidstone, Kent ME17 3DQ.

The CaF Directory of specific conditions and rare syndromes in children (including those that affect behaviour) with their family support networks can be obtained on subscription from Contact a Family, Equity House, 209–211 City Road, London EC1V 1JN.

Department for Education and Skills (DfES), Sanctuary Buildings, Great Smith Street, London SW1P 3BT
Tel: 0870 000 2288   Fax: 01928 794248   Email: info@dfes.gov.uk
Web site: www.dfes.gov.uk

The National Association for Special Educational Needs (NASEN),
4/5 Amber Business Village, Amber Close, Tamworth B77 4RP
Tel: 01827 311500   Fax: 01827 313005   Email: welcome@nasen.org.uk
Web site: www.nasen.org.uk

National Children's Bureau (NCB), 8 Wakley Street, London EC1V 1NG
Tel: 020 7843 6000   Fax: 020 7278 9512
Web site: www.ncb.org.uk

National Early Years Network (for customised in-house training), 77 Holloway Road, London N7 8JZ.

Qualifications and Curriculum Authority (QCA), 83 Piccadilly, London
W1J 8QA
Tel: 020 7509 5555   Fax: 020 7509 6666
Web site: www.qca.org.uk

QEd Publications, The Rom Building, Eastern Avenue, Lichfield, Staffs.
WS13 6RN
Tel: 01543 416353   Fax: 01543 419144   Email: orders@qed.uk.com
Web site: www.qed.uk.com

Save the Children *Working with Under Eights* (leaflets, books and training
on a wide range of issues including SEN) 17 Grove Lane, London SE5 8RD.